to

Erin & Joe

from

Liza Bailey

date

November 28, 2004

Snips and Snails

and puppy dog tails

Chrys Howard

PHOTOGRAPHY BY STACI ALBRITTON

HOWARD
PUBLISHING CO.

dedication

to my brothers, Kevin, Kerry, and Jeremy—
who let me take a glimpse into the world of boyhood

to my son, Ryan, and grandsons, John Luke, Asa, Will, and Maddox—
who let me continue the adventure

Our purpose at Howard Publishing is to:
Increase faith in the hearts of growing Christians
Inspire holiness in the lives of believers
Instill hope in the hearts of struggling people everywhere

Because He's coming again!

Snips and Snails and Puppy Dog Tails © 2001 Chrys Howard
All rights reserved. Printed in the United States of America

Published by Howard Publishing Co., Inc.,
3117 North 7th Street, West Monroe, LA 71291-2227

02 03 04 05 06 07 08 09 10   10 9 8 7 6 5 4 3 2

Interior design by LinDee Loveland
Photo hand tinting by Toni Worsham

Photography by Staci Albritton
Albritton Photography, 410 North 6th Street, West Monroe, LA 71291

Library of Congress Cataloging-in-Publication Data
Howard, Chrys, 1953–
Snips and snails and puppy dog tails / Chrys Howard ; photography by Staci Albritton.
p. cm.
ISBN 1-58229-161-6
1. Boys—Poetry. 2. Boys—Quotations, maxims, etc. I. Title: Snips and snails.
II. Albritton, Staci. III. Title.
PS3608.O9 S65 2001
811'.6—dc21   2001016707

Scriptures quoted from The Holy Bible, New Century Version, copyright © 1987, 1988, 1991 by
Word Publishing, Dallas, Texas 75234. Used by permission.

What are little boys made of?
What are little boys made of?
Frogs and snails
And puppy-dog tails,
That's what little boys are made of.

What are little girls made of?
What are little girls made of?
Sugar and spice
And all that's nice,
That's what little girls are made of.

Robert Southey, English poet
1774–1843

What are little boys made of?

Snips and snails and puppy dog tails

Daddies and cane poles

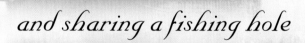

and sharing a fishing hole

Lizards and frogs

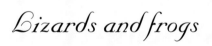

and balancing on logs

God made a world out of his dreams,
Of wondrous mountains, oceans, and streams,
Prairies and plains and wooded land,
Then paused and thought, "I need someone to stand
On top of the mountains, to conquer the seas,
Explore the plains and climb the trees,
Someone to start small and grow sturdy, strong like a tree."

He created boys, full of spirit and fun,
To explore and conquer, to romp and run,
With dirty faces, banged up chins,
With courageous hearts and boyish grins.
When He had completed the task He'd begun,
He said, "That's a job well done."

AUTHOR UNKNOWN

Boys are found everywhere—on top of, underneath, inside of,
climbing on, swinging from, running around, or jumping to.
Mothers love them, little girls hate them, older sisters and brothers tolerate them,
adults ignore them and Heaven protects them.

DALE EVANS ROGERS

Everything on earth, shout with joy to God!
Sing about his glory! Make his praise glorious!

Psalm 66:1–2

What are little boys made of?

Adventure and delight

and campfires at night

Laughter and charm and trips to the farm

I meant to do my work today—
But a brown bird sang in the apple tree,
And a butterfly flitted across the field,
And all the leaves were calling me.

And the wind went sighing over the land,
Tossing the grasses to and fro,
And a rainbow held out its shining hand—
So what could I do but laugh and go?

RICHARD LE GALLIENNE

There comes a time in every rightly constructed boy's life when he has a
raging desire to go somewhere and dig for hidden treasure.

MARK TWAIN

Let our sons in their youth grow like plants.

Psalm 144:12

What are little boys made of?

Bikes after school and playing it cool

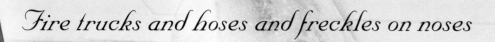

Fire trucks and hoses and freckles on noses

I'm not really sure
What I might grow up to be.
But I know that God has my plans—
He's holding them for me.

He's molding and He's shaping,
And I can't wait to see
The kind of person I'll become
And what God has planned for me.

Does He see me in an office
Sending out a fax?
Or maybe at a shopping mall
Figuring the tax?

Does He see me in an airplane
Flying high up above?
Or maybe I'm a preacher man
Sharing of God's love?

I guess I have to wait and see—
It's not as if I mind—
I'll gladly let God guide my steps
And follow close behind.

CHRYS HOWARD

The childhood shows the man, as morning shows the day.

JOHN MILTON, *Paradise Regained*

He has put his angels in charge of you
to watch over you wherever you go.

Psalm 91:11

What are little boys made of?

Helmets and hats and footballs and bats

Running and sliding

and tangled colliding

If I were very, very tall, as tall as I could be,
I'd play with all the little birds up in the topmost tree.
I'd jump right over houses and think nothing of a wall,
If I were very, very, very, very, very tall!

If I were very, very small, as small as I could be,
I'd run among the blades of grass where you could barely see;
I'd play with ants and beetles and I know I'd love them all.
If I were very, very, very, very, very small!

JOYCE L. BRISLEY

A child is a person who is going to carry on what you
have started.... The fate of humanity is in his hands.

ABRAHAM LINCOLN

The heavens tell the glory of God, and the skies
announce what his hands have made.

Psalm 19:1

What are little boys made of?

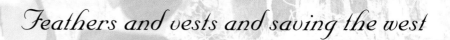

Feathers and vests and saving the west

Dragons and dinosaurs

and guards for castle doors

I'll get a rope and grab a hat
And put some boots on me
Then I can be most anything
I could dream to be.

Even though it's make-believe,
It's fun just the same
To pretend for just a while;
I know it's just a game.

Yesterday I was Superman;
Today I'm Daniel Boone.
Tomorrow I will climb a tree
And fly up to the moon.

CHRYS HOWARD

Keep your eyes on the stars and your feet on the ground.

THEODORE ROOSEVELT

Human life is like grass; we grow like a flower in the field.

Psalm 103:15

What are little boys made of?

Friendship and fun and enjoying the sun

Wiggles and haircuts and giggles and funny looks

A child to hold and cuddle,
'Tis a gift from God above.
And the world is so much brighter,
When you have a child to love.

AUTHOR UNKNOWN

God makes the world all over again whenever a little child is born.

JEAN PAUL RICHTER

I praise you because you made me in an amazing and wonderful way.
What you have done is wonderful. I know this very well.

Psalm 139:14

What are little boys made of?

Hugs and kisses and middle-of-the-night wishes

Toys and bears

and sweet good-night prayers

That's what little boys are made of.

Each second we live is a new and unique moment
Of the universe, a moment that will never be again...
And what do we teach our children?...
We should say to each of them: do you know what you are?
You are a marvel. You are unique.
In all the years that have passed, there has never been another child like you.
Your legs, your arms, your clever fingers, the way you move.
You may become a Shakespeare, a Michelangelo, a Beethoven.
You have the capacity for anything. Yes, you are a marvel.

PABLO CASALS

Chrys Howard (the second woman from the left) is the creator and author of *Sugar and Spice and Everything Nice*. Chrys lives in West Monroe, Louisiana, with her husband, John. They have three grown children—Korie, Ryan, and Ashley—and nine grandchildren—John Luke, Sadie, Macy, Asa, Ally, Will, Maddox, Aslyn, and Bella. Holding a degree in elementary education, Chrys spent ten years teaching children with learning differences. She currently directs a Christian youth camp, works with her family's business, speaks at ladies and youth seminars, and spends lots of time with her grandkids.

Staci Albritton (the first woman from the right) brought the magic and excitement of photography to this book. She lives in West Monroe, Louisiana, with her two children, Calli and Casey. A second-generation photographer, specializing in children's portraits, Staci is a recognized professional in her field.

LinDee Loveland (the woman on the back row) is employed by Howard Publishing Company as senior graphic designer. LinDee's unique creative talents and skillful study of design make each page of this book an adventure. LinDee; her husband, William; and two boys, Hunter and Travis, live in Calhoun, Louisiana.